EDITION

HOW TO FILL YOUR SMALL BUSINESS WITH NON-STOP CUSTOMERS, MONEY, SUCCESS AND GROWTH...

LEAVE EVERY SINGLE ONE OF YOUR COMPETITORS SCRATCHING THEIR HEADS DOWN TO THE BONE...

AND CREATE GREAT, GREAT PERSONAL WEALTH QUICKLY!

PAUL GUNTER AND **ANDREW SHORTEN**

SQUARE MILE PUBLICATIONS
London

First published 2009 in London, United Kingdom by Square Mile Publications Ltd.

2nd print edition 2011 by Square Mile Publications Ltd.

Printed and bound by the MPG Books Group in the UK

ISBN: 978-0-9562787-0-8

Catalogue Data:

Gunter, Paul
Shorten, Andrew
    How To Fill Your Small Business With Non-Stop Customers, Money, Success
    And Growth... Leave Every Single One Of Your Competitors Scratching Their
    Heads Down To The Bone... And Create Great, Great Personal Wealth Quickly!

    1. Business Success   2. Strategy   3. Marketing

Square Mile Publications Ltd provides books at trade and other special discounts to use as premiums, sales promotions, or for use in training programmes.

For further information write or email to:
Sales Manager, Square Mile Publications Ltd.
2nd Floor, 145-157 St John Street
London EC1V 4PY
service@squaremilepublications.com

PRIVATE BUSINESS SUCCESS & MARKETING CONSULTANCY
You can consult with Paul Gunter & Andrew Shorten privately to help mastermind specific business success and marketing strategies for your business or professional practice. To receive details, please write to them c/o Square Mile Publications Ltd at the address above or telephone 0845 310 2467.

This book is dedicated to all of the business owners and entrepreneurs who believe in, and achieve, their dreams.

With thanks to all of our friends and family, colleagues, clients and students who have, taught, encouraged, supported and inspired us to achieve.

"This is a book about developing a marketing mindset. Before you spend a single penny on your advertising campaign, customer acquisition strategy or indeed any marketing effort... read this book! It contains the essential fundamentals which underpin every marketing activity."

Richard Parkes Cordock
EnterpriseLeaders.com

"Paul and Andrew really get under the skin of what makes a great business tick; they understand that so much about it is attitude - towards your customers, towards marketing and towards yourself. A recommended read."

Jonathan Jay
SuccessTrackOnline.com

"Paul and Andrew have identified the seven areas that make or break business - and yet which so few small businesses ever get right. The shocking statistics they reveal highlight this sad fact.

If your business isn't living up to expectations, if your cash flow isn't flowing, and if you find it hard to attract new customers or clients and generate streams of ongoing sales, then I strongly urge you to buy this powerful yet quick-to-read book and discover seven of the most important lessons you'll ever learn as an entrepreneur."

Ed Rivis
Author of The Ultimate Web Marketing Strategy

"I found "How To Fill Your Small Business With Non-Stop Customers, Money, Success And Growth" a very interesting and informative read that had me nodding my head in agreement the whole way through, in fact my copy of the book now has underlines and markings where I made my own notes.

This book is from two entrepreneurs whom have actually been there and done it and not just written a book full of theory and hypothetical situations.

I highly recommend this book for anyone considering going into business for themselves or if already in business - it is a must read if you are thinking about taking your business to the next level."

Nick James
Nick-James.com

"Paul and Andrew are right on the money with this book. If you follow their instructions you won't go far wrong."

Wendy Dashwood-Quick
Personal Development and Career Coach

"In this book, Paul and Andrew set forth simple, yet essential and very powerful business principles that work! Success in business is about your customers and not about you! Passion and attitude are key! And a positive cash flow is of utmost importance! These are just a few of the 'gems' you will learn in this easy to read book.

Although our business efforts have been quite successful, as a former public school teacher I've never taken a business or marketing course in my life. Our principles have been guided by personal experience, instinct and building positive relationships.

It's great to be reaffirmed that we've been doing the right things!
'Stacks and stacks' of thanks to Paul and Andrew for their inspiring book!"

Bob Fox
Founder and President, Speed Stacks, Inc. SpeedStacks.com

"Paul and Andrew have managed to simplify what can be a complex subject and the result is a fantastic overview of what it takes to succeed in business. Information on a variety of topics, some of which are so often overlooked by other 'business authors', including the importance of prosperity consciousness, why your business must provide extraordinary customer service and why you need a game plan not a business plan.

In today's world it takes more than traditional business skills to succeed and this book can help you achieve your 'game plan' fast."

Diane Johnston
NetStarSolutions.co.uk

"If you want to give your business momentum and are on the lookout for new ideas to bring about change then you are taking the first step by reading this book. Paul and Andrew have outlined the ideas to make any business successful and ones that can be applied to any industry. Best of all they show you that by having a passion for your business you will have the greatest chance of succeeding!"

Dr. Faiz Kermani

Contents

About The Authors

Paul Gunter and Andrew Shorten are driven to show serious-minded entrepreneurs how virtually any small business holds the potential to exponentially grow and become abundantly rich.

They both possess an inherent ability to identify rapid and substantial opportunity in virtually every business they look at.

They show that when you understand how to optimise every activity your business performs, and when you discover how to ethically influence customers or clients in their droves to buy from you - rather than your less savvy and knowledgeable competitors - you can soon dominate your marketplace. Then you can build a business that not only becomes the obvious choice for your customers to buy from, but rewards you with rapid and large financial returns.

Introduction

Success in business is a principle that can be applied by anyone willing to spend time learning how to use it. Generally however, that principle, known as the law of success, is the exact opposite of what you normally see being done in the business world.

Don't believe us? If you take a look at the state of businesses in general, you will see that approximately 76 per cent of start-up businesses fail within their first five years. The vast majority of those that go out of business failed to firstly build the correct foundations, and then employ all of the principles and strategies that lead to business success. Look at any ultra successful business and it will be evident that they are applying most of the secrets revealed within this book.

A little pointer before we move on. We are sharing with you our greatest business success secrets and experience. We urge you to read and apply everything you learn from this book. If you do, then your business will flourish. If you don't, you will never reach your full potential - and the worst offenders will fail before they've even started.

Read this book with an open mind and let's get straight on with building your business!

CHAPTER 1

The Secret To Exponential Growth That 99% Of Businesses Overlook

"The secret of success is constancy to purpose."
Benjamin Disraeli - British Prime Minister and Author

It is crucial that you are focused on the primary purpose behind your business. This primary purpose will elevate you and your business above your competitors and will ultimately lead to your success. With this primary purpose at the forefront of your mind, you will always succeed. If you want to succeed, you will make it possible when you instill this into every action, every communication, every product or service you provide, every thought, every detail and thing you do in your business.

If you don't instill this primary purpose within your business, you will struggle and never reach full potential.

Your Primary Purpose

The primary purpose of every business, regardless of size, is to provide the highest level of service, benefit, and result to the people who enquire, ask for advice and buy from you. This is your utmost purpose as a business owner or entrepreneur and this should be your mission.

Your business's success has nothing to do with your desire to attain success, money and freedom. These personal achievements are one or more of the major reasons you have created your business in the first place, and they are important reasons. But remember, they should not be, and cannot be, the primary purpose.

Your primary purpose absolutely must be to serve every person who comes to you, at the very highest and best level you and your business can provide.

It is all and only about them, your customers, and not you. Your desire to attain success, money and freedom has no influence at all on what will draw customers or clients to you and your business. The ultimate reason that a customer will be attracted to you is the benefit and result that you can provide to them from your product or service.

When you focus on this you will discover the power of word of mouth and referral. Potential customers will be naturally drawn to you in larger numbers. There is no more powerful endorsement than a highly satisfied customer. Whether they praise your rapid response and delivery times, or your willingness to answer questions and give honest answers, or your after sales service; the result is the same. You have gained a loyal customer who can't wait to tell others about how good you are.

Take a minute to imagine your business right now and then imagine, with limitless possibility, morphing your business into the best it can be when you put the primary purpose behind each and every improvement. Imagine that people can't get better value or a more satisfying result from anywhere else – you are the best of the best in every respect. You see, if this was for real, and it can be, everyone will talk about your unique caring attitude, your unique interest in them, your mission to provide them always with the best possible result. Everyone who wants what you sell, or provide, will flock to you in droves. When this happens your business will be unstoppable and your success glorious. And then, and only then, can your goals of success, money and freedom be achieved.

A bonus and by product of having achieved this, is that you get to feel really good about what you're doing, and so will your employees. This is rarely experienced in the business world. Getting positive feedback makes everyone feel good, and perform better, which in turn makes you more effective and efficient.

Remind yourself and your staff every single day of your primary purpose and other goals. Consider every action you take in your everyday business activities, whether it is with your customers, staff or suppliers, and ensure that your primary purpose is in every detail.

Just do this and your customers will recognise what you are doing for them. The result will be their ongoing lifetime custom and recommendation of your business for years to come.

CHAPTER 2

How Your Attitude And Mindset Has Total Influence Over Your Future

"Success is not the key to happiness.
Happiness is the key to success.
If you love what you are doing, you will be successful."
Albert Schweitzer – Nobel Prize Winner

Your attitude is the main reason for your failure or success in achieving everything you want in business. You are solely responsible - and that can be a daunting thought – but it is also a wonderfully positive thing to know that you can, by your attitude, affect your business. We want you to do this only in a positive way and that's what we want you to understand from this chapter. By changing the way you think, by believing in yourself, and bringing true passion to everything you do, you can achieve success.

Passion

Back to your primary purpose – why are you in business? You can't underestimate the importance of knowing why you are doing what you do. Of course you want to make money – it isn't a business in the true sense of the word if you are not doing so – but that must not be your only motivation. Want to be an 'instant millionaire' and don't care how you do it? Then you might make some money, but real success never comes from doing something just for the money. That attitude cannot sustain growth or real success and although naturally we all want money and what it can do for us, you must remember what we said in that first chapter and focus on your customers.

Putting the principle of primary purpose first is not a 'soft option' or a woolly kind of approach to business. It is the most effective and sustainable way to build a really great and successful business. If your only focus is money, you are always going to be looking for ways to squeeze extra profit or cut costs, and that is the surest way to make your customers feel undervalued. Great customer service is not an optional extra, it is the foundation of a successful business, but if you start thinking of sending goods out second class instead of first class, or cutting your response time to customer emails so they may not get a reply for several days, then you are not making them feel good about you, and your business. Treat them as being of the highest level of importance to you and spend time, money and effort on improving your customer service and you will see great results.

It is that simple, but that level of customer service and satisfaction only comes when you are passionate about what you are doing – not about the bottom line. 'Do what you love and the money will follow' is the title of a book by US author Marsha Sinetar and it sums up what we are saying. If you put your abilities and skills behind doing something you love and are passionate about, then not only will it bring you success, but also a far greater feeling of satisfaction than just pursuing profit alone can ever do.

If you just want to shift as much product as possible to make the most money out of it, then by all means do so. But, if you want to build a successful and sustainable business you won't be able to provide a long-term platform of service and customer satisfaction just by focusing on profit. Bring your focus to the passion you have for your business and just watch your business grow.

Entrepreneurialism

Working for yourself is one of the most rewarding things you can do, both financially and on a personal level. You will have your reasons why you want to run your own business, but generally the main one most people mention is the desire to take control of their lives. To be able to act as they wish, not as their boss tells them to, and to have responsibility for the decisions and actions they take.

The biggest benefits you get from running your own business are ones that are denied to large corporations. You are making the decisions and you can act on them immediately. Anyone who has ever worked in the corporate world knows how slow the process is from a new idea being introduced to it being implemented, and how very frustrating that can be.

When you run your own business you are uniquely placed to spot market trends and immediately act on them. You can keep developing new products or services and test market them before a large corporation has even discussed the idea. Success in business is about staying ahead, and you do that by being able to respond immediately to market changes and emerging trends.

Your customers want their needs met immediately, and you can do that. You don't have to run it past the R&D department, the Product Development Manager, The Production Manager or the Marketing People because you combine those roles. Remember what we said about customer satisfaction? You are able to really capitalise on your relationship with your customers by showing that you are listening to what they want, asking them for feedback and then presenting that to them in new products and services. Why wouldn't they be impressed by that and, more importantly, respond by giving you their continued custom and sales.

Innovation is often mentioned as the key trait in entrepreneurial businesses, and that's what your customers are looking for. They don't want yesterday's products and services, they may accept today's version if there's nothing else, but what they always want is tomorrow's product, now. Be entrepreneurial and recognise that you are in a very powerful position compared to those stuck in the corporate environment.

Self Belief And Confidence

We don't mean the 'I am a great businessman' type of confidence; we mean the level of deep belief in yourself that is the mark of true confidence. In order to succeed in business you must have a deep confidence in your own ability and in who you are. Failure in any walk of life can often be traced to poor self-esteem or lack of confidence to succeed, and this is nowhere more true than in running your own business. You don't have the backing and support that a major corporation has, it is all down to you and you need a level of psychological robustness to cope when things are not going well – and that can happen to any business from time to time.

Being confident is not just an attitude or a pose; when you really believe you can achieve something then you are more likely to do so than if you doubt it. In fact, we would go so far as to say that Henry Ford, the US car manufacturer got it right when he said:

"If you think you can do a thing or think you can't do a thing, you're right."

So it's better to be positive and believe in yourself to create the right conditions for the thing you desire to happen.

Not sure you are able to 'think yourself successful'? Well you can certainly think yourself into failure by dwelling on what you can't do, or believe you can't do, so isn't it worth a try? Sometimes we can believe that what we want to achieve isn't really manageable, or we don't have the ability or talent to pull it off. Many of the philosophical schools of the last century addressed this problem, particularly those like the Christian Scientists and Science of Mind, and their studies led them to firmly believe that if you had what they called a 'true desire' then you also must already have the ability to achieve it within you. Your true desire lies in that inner confidence that you need to make things happen. You must develop that confidence so that things come to you more easily, you generate a state of mind that puts other people at their ease and makes them confident in you and your ability to do what you promise.

Another great American businessman, Walt Disney, summed it up, if you are still having any doubts:

"If you can dream it, you can do it."

He was the man who more than anyone brought dreams to life, so if your dream is to run a successful business you have the ability to do it. Is it guaranteed? Of course not, because along with ability you also need focus, dedication and hard work, but add those into the mix and it's hard to see how you could fail.

All you have to do is trust yourself, believe in what you want to achieve, and always act as if you have already got there.

Prosperity Consciousness

What do you think about money? That may seem a strange question; but what you think about money will dictate how much of it you can create. This follows on from what we just talked about in relation to your confidence, and relates to something called 'poverty consciousnesses'. You can feel rich on a low income and poor as a millionaire; it's not the money it's how you think about it. If you want to read more about this, take a look at the book called 'Rich Dad, Poor Dad', by Robert Kiyosaki that sums this philosophy up better than most.

Basically, if you think poor, you stay poor, because your actions follow your thoughts – as they do with your confidence levels. Conversely, if you have the attitude and thoughts of a rich person, you will attract more money to you. If you see yourself enjoying a rich lifestyle, and consciously spend time around the people, places and things that represent that to you, then you will subconsciously start acting as if you are in the right place. You will be relaxed and confident around money and that makes it easier to attain it.

Whatever the economic situation in the world, there is always an abundant supply of money. Some people may not have any, but others have a lot and if you trust in that then why shouldn't some of it be yours – as much as you want?

Your attitude is all important: the American self-development author Louise Hay makes this crystal clear in her book 'You Can Heal your Life' where she gives a wonderful exercise that will help you assess your own attitude to money and abundance. Just for a moment imagine yourself standing in front of a huge infinite ocean. It represents wealth and money and you are allowed to go down to the water and take what you want. See yourself doing that and then notice what you have taken – did you just cup your hands and scoop it up, did you have a bucket or a pipeline or nothing at all? If you only think you deserve the wealth that can be held in your hands, then that is what you will get.

Innovation
You don't have to be 'creative' to have a creative approach. All great companies have been started by people with a great idea, one that they looked at from every angle and then moved beyond it to territory unknown. That's what Steve Jobs did at Apple, and it's what you will be doing if you are running a successful business.

Thinking outside the box has become a bit of a cliché, but like all clichés it is based on truth. You can develop yourself into a creative thinker, problem solver, product developer and salesman, and you will find it a lot more interesting than just looking at any situation from only one angle.

Being creative in your approach is about not taking anything at face value, but looking under, behind, and around it to see what else might be there. That way you will discover insights and inspiration you can then pass on to your customers – and they will be grateful for it.

If you're offering a service or product don't just make your mind up that it is 'the greatest in the world' but spend time exploring what makes it great, why it works, who it works for, who it doesn't work for. The key is in the questioning, and the more you ask the more valuable the information you get – even if the answers don't seem to make any sense at the time, write everything down and keep coming back to that list. It's a resource for you to explore and gives you a new angle on something that may be all-too familiar to you, and again that is something you can pass on to your customers.

A creative approach will intrigue your customers – it isn't exactly what they were expecting and so they pay more attention to it. It's where you can let your passion for your product or service really take off and give you a whole new approach to your marketing. Do you use the same phrase in your headlines or adverts or describe your product in exactly the same way each time? If you do, then you run the risk of people just not reading them because they are so familiar. If you mix it up with plenty of variety then they will pay attention.

Got too many problems to bother about being creative? Then you will continue to have them, because the only way to deal with problems is to turn them on their head and put your energy behind finding the solution. That is the creative approach and it will pay you dividends. Think again about Steve Jobs; Apple a few years ago was in serious trouble but Jobs, despite the accountants wailing in his ears, didn't spend time trying to market the Mac more aggressively. Instead he focused on a new innovation; he thought about his customers and who they were and what they liked – it was change and innovation. Out of that crisis came the iPod and later the iPhone, brand new concepts that took the world by storm. You may not be inventing the next iPod, but you will certainly have innovative solutions in your business if you just focus on what your customers most want and need, and find a way to give it to them.

Your business, like all others, will go through challenging times. Your willingness to take a creative approach to your problems could be the greatest opportunity for growth you'll ever get. Don't let challenges overwhelm or defeat you, but treat them like an amazingly interesting puzzle – and one you can solve. It may not come immediately, but if you just keep thinking and brainstorming and throwing ideas around then a solution will come – and don't dismiss it just because it seems crazy – remember, that's what they said about the iPod.

CHAPTER 3

Why Your Game Plan Should Be At The Forefront Of Your Business Strategy

"The tragedy in life doesn't lie in not reaching your goal.
The tragedy lies in having no goal to reach."
Benjamin Mays – Mentor to Martin Luther King

You must absolutely have a game plan. We don't mean sit down and write a formal business plan with all types of financial spreadsheets in it. You know, the type that bank mangers demand before they lend you money. We mean your general plan and goals for your business in order to maximise your success. The famous American inventor Thomas Edison certainly got it right when he said:

"Good fortune is what happens when opportunity meets with planning."

Or to put it another way, if you fail to plan then you plan to fail. If you went into a railway station and asked for a ticket you would be asked your destination, and if you didn't know you could always buy a ticket for a certain value and you would get somewhere – but it almost certainly wouldn't be where you really wanted to be. It is exactly the same in your business and you need to know the answers to these three key questions:

- What do you want to achieve?
- Where do you want your business to be in 1, 3, and 5 years time?
- How do you plan to develop it?

Most businesses start from an idea, and it is all too easy to be caught up in the excitement of the idea and the buzz of starting a new business. Somehow the running of the business seems to take over and it becomes all about dealing on a day to day basis with all the things that need to be done. That is the classic mistake most business owners and entrepreneurs make. They spend all their time working *in* their business, solving problems, fulfilling orders and so on. What you must also be doing is working *on* your business in terms of marketing, product development and future planning.

You may be familiar with the Harry Potter books series? They follow the adventures of the boy wizard through his seven years at Hogwart's School. J K Rowling, who wrote the seven book series, has said that before she wrote a word of the first novel, she knew the plot for the last one – and all the ones in between. In other words, she planned the whole thing and although she made some changes on the way, her initial plan for the plots of all seven novels survived pretty much intact. Her planning paid off; with over 250 million copies sold worldwide she saw her strategy implemented and gained the success she deserved. Do you think she would have done as well if she just started to write and didn't have a clue where she was going to end up?

To go back to those three questions we just asked you: unless you know what you want to achieve with your business and its future growth and development then you will not achieve the success you are looking for.

You must clearly be able to state your goals for the business because unless you do then everyone else – including your customers – won't understand what you stand for and you won't be able to build good relationships with them. Remember that example of just buying a ticket with no stated destination? How are you going to build a strong market share, or dominate your niche, if you don't have a clear destination or end result in mind?

Your goals must be clearly defined for you to achieve them. They must be **SMART** goals:

Specific – how many customers do you want to have? What turnover or market position do you want to achieve?

Measurable – it must be able to have a benchmark to check on your progress, so not 'lots of customers' but '100 more a month' is measurable.

Achievable – if 100 customers a month are possible, then great, but you must be able to fulfil that number to the same standard as your present customer base.

Realistic – can you really gain 100 customers a month or is that a dream? If gaining 50 customers is more likely then don't inflate the figures but stay with a realistic estimate of what you can achieve.

Timely – when do you want those customers by? The last day in the current month or in 3 months time? Put a time deadline on your goals so you know what you have to achieve.

In other words, you must be able to see that you are achieving your goals in a stated time frame, in a way that you know you can manage and in a way that you can maintain over the required period of time. Be as specific as you possibly can. Just saying 'I want to be successful' means nothing in terms of goal achievement. If you say 'I want to be the market leader in my niche within 12 months' then that is a clear goal. If you follow this simple goal setting formula – one that was made popular by Sir John Whitmore, the man the Independent newspaper rated as the Number One Business Coach - then you will reap the benefits in terms of success, sales and the sustainability of your business.

SMART is also applied to another well-used business maxim; that you need to work smarter, not harder. That can only be done through planning and by being excited and energised by the goals you are setting for your business and yourself. Don't just write your goals down and forget them, keep them in prominent view, carry them around with you and keep reading them. Sound silly? Well that's what some of the world's most successful global entrepreneurs do. They do it because they know that by constantly reminding themselves of their goals, their every action and thought is naturally geared towards achieving them. It works for them, it works for us and it will certainly work for you too.

Because you are your business in a very real sense, it also pays you to create personal goals too. Define what you want for yourself, whether that is a specific type of car, or a place to go on holiday, or anything else. If you want 'more money', be very specific and put a number on it – if you want a million pounds, then that's what you need to be planning for. Let yourself really enjoy thinking about what you want for yourself, and along with your business goals spend time each day just reminding yourself of them and seeing how you are moving towards achieving them.

CHAPTER 4

The Two Most Important Factors That Will Ensure Your Long-Term Survival

"Having no profit is like a cancer, you die very slowly. You can run businesses without a profit, but you'll slowly perish, and having no cash-flow is like a heart attack. You're dead. The business is bust."
Theo Paphitis – Entrepreneur and Dragon

Cash Flow Is King

One key to running a successful business is to understand that cash flow is the life blood of all businesses and you cannot operate without it. However brilliant your ideas, products or services, unless you have cash flow to support them you will fail. If you are out of cash then you are out of business – it is that simple.

If you don't control your cash flow, then it will control you and that can be disastrous. You don't need to be a whiz with figures; if you can't manage your finances yourself then you *must* find someone who can look after your cash for you. We are not saying you need to have lots of cash floating around, but you have to be able to look after the cash you do have and make sure it is enough to keep your business viable.

You may have a warehouse full of goods that are valued at a million pounds, but if you only have £50 in the bank you don't have cash flow, you have assets that need cash to move them out of there. If you don't have enough cash flow to pay for their shipping, packing and postage, then you are heading for disaster. It sounds obvious, but many people have plenty of money tied up in stock or property and not enough to pay their bills. Don't let that be you.

To create a successful business you need to have a healthy cash flow so you can utilise it to create more wealth and success. Life is full of unexpected problems, and business is no exception. You need to have a 'rainy day' fund to bail you out if a large client doesn't pay their bills, or you get paid after 6 weeks on a large job instead of the 3 weeks you agreed. If the economy takes a nosedive, or something unexpected happens to your supply chain, or your traditional market ceases to exist, you need to have a cushion. You must have a financial safety net so that you can stay in business when times are bad and the cash you have put aside for this will help you stay afloat when your competitors are going bust. Remember, you don't go broke if you look after your cash flow but if you ignore it then you almost certainly will go under.

Focus On Profit Not Turnover

When starting a business it's very easy to get excited about numbers. You focus on how many items you have sold, or the number of new customers you have gained and that can delude you into thinking you are successful. It's not the number of items sold, but the profit on each one that matters. It's not having 500 customers, but knowing exactly what each one brings you in terms of profit. Before you put a price on a product or service you must think about what your profit is and whether that gives the customer good value. Get that balance right and you will succeed.

Sadly, too many businesses concentrate on turnover and not profit. It sounds great to have a business that turns over £2 million a year, but there is no benefit if you make zero profit on it. Much more successful is a business that turns over £150k and makes £100k profit. You are in business to make money, and unless you know what your profit margin is you have no hope of doing that successfully.

Many businesses fail to pay attention to this very simple fact: if you haven't accurately assessed your profit margin then you won't be charging for your product or service at a rate that will make you money. If that's what you are doing, then you are on your way to losing money and your business.

CHAPTER 5

How To Leave Your Competitors Scratching Their Heads Down To The Bone

"One customer, well taken care of, could be more
valuable than $10,000 worth of advertising"
Jim Rohn - Entrepreneur, Author, and Motivational
Speaker

When you have Chapters 1 and 2 covered, you will be well on your way to turning your customers into a virtual and no-cost sales force. If they are happy with your product or service they will enthusiastically 'sell' you to others and there is no more powerful persuader than a genuine word of mouth recommendation.

Every satisfied customer has the potential to bring you in new leads and more sales, so it makes sense to do all you can in terms of customer service to make them keep coming back to you.

Never take them for granted and always go the extra mile in terms of service, bonuses and contact so they feel valued and respected. It goes without saying that you must give them value, but it is the way you treat them that will make them feel like they are the most important customer in the world to you. Unless you treat your customers well and form a good relationship with them, you lose. Create a sense of loyalty and enthusiasm in them and you win – and keep on winning.

The overriding principle of maximising your sales and profitability is to take care of your existing customers as if they were gold, because they are. It will cost you far less to resell to the customers that you already have, rather than having to find new ones. One of the best known business principles is the 80/20 rule. That's the one where the ratio always is constant between those two figures so you can count on the fact that 20% of your customer base will provide 80% of your bottom line profit.

You need to have simple yet effective methods in place to ensure your customers have a positive perception of you, and your product or service, so they keep coming back for more. Being 'customer focused' and just satisfying customers or clients is not enough in today's market, you also have to understand them and how they operate. Every interaction between you and your customer is critical. You have to know how they think, be able to realise exactly what they want, need, and are looking for. You also need to manage the way you deal with them in a way that makes sure you also get what you want. It's only when you really understand how these interactions work that you can use them to not only build customer confidence and loyalty, but also to win their hearts and minds. In other words, you need to create customers that *want* to deal *only* with you and not your competition.

There are some key points in achieving all of this, and all of them are fairly obvious, though sadly that doesn't mean everyone places the value on them that they ought to. Your first priority is to actually find your customers and then do everything you can to turn them into a happy repeat customer.

Lead generation is a whole separate topic that you will find covered in depth in most marketing books, so we won't go over it here. Assuming you have customers then you should focus your attention on making their buying experience with you an absolute pleasure. The first thing to do is make their interaction with you easy, pleasurable and from a position of great customer service. Be your customers 'trusted advisor'.

All businesses should provide the right product, deliver as promised and do it promptly. The key here which will set you apart from your competitors is to add value and over-deliver. Talk to your customers to find out exactly what they need and make them feel that you really value their input and take their suggestions seriously.

Make sure you, and all staff members who come into contact with a customer, are genuinely interested in what they want and will put their needs first by paying real attention to them. This is not a hard selling approach, because people won't keep coming back to you if it is. Your profit is best and most easily made by selling over and over again through retaining customer loyalty. It is all about making the customer feel special. If you can do that by making the experience better for the customer then they will only want to buy from you, and not your competitors.

It's key to your success that you keep the customer satisfied, not just pay lip service to it. The customer knows the difference between someone who is genuinely being helpful and ensuring they get what they want, and someone who is just out for a sale. Great service is how you win customer loyalty, and customer loyalty is your advantage over your competition.

The benefit of customer loyalty is that it's a catalyst to the exponential growth of your customer base. A personal recommendation is the most powerful sales endorsement you can get. It's another reason to do everything you can to make sure your customers become part of your army of happy customers.

Don't Sell Yourself Short

Whatever product or service you sell, you have to make sure your customers can immediately recognise what's in it for them, so make sure you get across what your features, advantages and benefits are. Usually these are obvious to you, but they may not be to your customers, and if not then you are missing an opportunity.

In the end, what you think about your business doesn't matter; it's what the customer thinks that is important. Ask them, and pay real attention to their answers. Customers are looking for reliability and consistency so that they get exactly what they ordered, each time they order it. If you get feedback about poor delivery then immediately find out what the problem was and fix it. And don't forget to thank, or reward, your customers for bringing problems to your attention.

The Next Step

Just making a sale is not enough, in fact we go further and say don't make a sale unless you have more to offer after your customer has committed to buy. The reason is simple, that's the point at which they are most ready to buy again and in the frame of mind to do so. If you don't have a product to up-sell or cross-sell to them you really are missing a great opportunity. But, you are not pressure selling to them, you are making recommendations to help them and this will increase your authority and relationship with them.

We go into more detail about all these points in our business marketing book (www.businessmarketingbook.com), but we have given you an outline of the most important area of business success in this chapter.

CHAPTER 6

Find And Nurture An Extraordinary Team To Take Your Business To The Top

"Some people have greatness thrust upon them.
Very few have excellence thrust upon them."
John W. Gardner – Former US Secretary of Health
and Author

No man is an island, and no business succeeds unless you build a good support team around you. It's vital that you know your competencies as well as your strengths and weaknesses. No one can do everything equally well, and although you may be a brilliant product developer you might not be a good manager or comfortable with finance. When you are ready to expand your business, it's important to get all the right skills working together in your business by picking staff and teams who fulfil those roles.

Whether your business employs 2 or 200 people you still have to cover all the skill bases, just like a football team. The greatest football team in the world must still have a goal keeper, defenders, midfielders and strikers who are the best in their individual positions. Success would not be achieved by having an unbalanced team of 11 defenders and a business doesn't run only on ideas people, you must have the production, marketing and finance positions covered too.

You need the right people in the right positions in the right team and when you have that, the job still isn't over. You also have to respect, value and reward your employees by listening to, teaching, inspiring and incentivising them.

Keep the good ones and promote the best.

Finding Your Superstars

If you want the best staff, you have to know exactly what you want and what you need from them. Sadly, most people waste money on recruitment adverts or agencies because they are too general in what they are looking for. It comes down to one simple fact; you must be 100% specific about your requirements. It is only by doing so that you will attract the sort of people you are looking for; the ones who are just right for your business, not the ones that will probably be just ok.

It wastes both your time and your money if you don't spell out exactly what your requirements are. A more general advert will probably bring in more responses, but you don't want 100 applicants who *might do*, you just want the one or two who are perfect. You may get fewer applicants, but they will be the right type and they will see from your ad whether they are the perfect fit for the job.

Not sure how to do it? Here is an example of a clearly written and specific advert for an office manager, and you can use it as a template for pretty much any position by just adjusting some of the wording.

**EXCEPTIONAL OFFICE MANAGER WANTED
FOR GROWING ONLINE BUSINESS**

Good basic salary plus generous performance pay. Earn up to £40k a year.
Rapid growth means we want a smart office manager who loves their work and takes pride in doing an EXTRAORDINARY job. Superb training and support provided.

You will have full responsibility for your position and be rewarded above basic salary for high quality and reliable work. Call between 9.30am and 12.30pm, Monday-Wednesday and tell us why you are our next superstar office manager.
(Telephone number and email contact details)

This advert is clear, specific and will frighten off anyone who is looking to just coast through a job. This advert asks candidates to contact you on specific days at a specific time for a good reason. It will tell you if they can follow instructions – if they can't, why would you want to employ them?

Rewarding Excellence With Pay-On-Performance

You may think that just paying someone a good salary is enough; but you are wrong. If you want dedicated, enthusiastic and effective staff you need to reward them by making it possible for them to earn a much bigger salary by performing at their best.

The key word here is 'earn', because most companies don't reward their staff for exceptional effort and performance. They give them a good basic wage, and a small bonus or commission which puts staff in the mindset that they don't need to do more than the minimum amount. Why should they if they are going to get their basic wage anyway, no matter how excellent their performance - or how average? That's the wrong message to give out. And the wrong pay structure.

The secret is to create individual or small group 'niches' within your business. Each individual, or small team, is responsible for their work or projects and is paid on successful completion or on the sustained high degree of performance they achieve every day and every hour. This means that the majority of each person's pay is performance-pay, or bonus, or commission. Whatever you want to call it, it's based on performance and nothing less. When their performance is well rewarded then, and only then, do employees take responsibility for their own salary.

Furthermore, they enjoy it because there's far greater satisfaction from knowing that the majority of money and recognition is a direct result of their own actual performance. Far greater satisfaction than there ever is from a monthly wage that is given no matter what performance has been delivered. As a business owner or entrepreneur you receive revenue and profit that is totally dependent on your business performance and as a result of providing service and value. If you fail to provide at least an acceptable level of service, value and results, your business will suffer and your customers will soon stop coming to you. Your staff must learn to think like this as well, so that if they perform well they receive optimum reward and if they fail to perform, they fail to receive that reward.

This approach works and is extremely simple. It's no secret that people do enjoy being given autonomy and trust to achieve what you ask of them.

Helping Staff To Become Exceptional
Anyone starting a new job will remember their first day as a mixture of anticipation and nervousness. It's your job to make that first day the blueprint for how your staff will work with you, and how you will make sure you have exceptional staff. First impressions count and are everlasting so make sure you get it right.

They are going to want to impress you, but it is also up to you to give them the right first impression and demonstrate an environment of organisation, efficiency, enjoyment, commitment, motivation and focus. With this, your new member of staff will need to feel that they can achieve a quick and impressive start so give them the tools they need for the job.

Running a business is time consuming, and it can easily lead to you not paying enough time and attention into making your new staff welcome, and in developing their skills and talents with ongoing training. That's a major mistake because new staff then need to know what their role is in your company, and how they can see their future developing. If they are not properly welcomed and integrated into your company, and know what is expected of them, then how can they possibly bring their performance up to an extraordinary level? The answer is they don't. In fact you may have wasted your money in recruiting them as they can become bored and feel stifled and start searching for a job that is more fulfilling.

Two essential elements that must be present are a genuine welcome from you, and a clear outline of the training they are going to receive. Whether you train them personally, or bring in an external company, you must make clear what kind of training they can expect and what it will lead to. People respond to having their needs met, untrained staff can feel insecure in their job, and they want to have the right training to do a good job. They certainly won't do an excellent one without it and the better you train them then the greater the edge you give your business, and this certainly gives you an advantage over your competitors.

Maintaining Training

Training someone is not a one-off activity, but a continuous commitment to maintain and improve skills and effectiveness. Staff development depends on you giving them ongoing additional and refresher training as it is needed. Fulfilment comes from developing new skills and tools, and that is something that everyone wants from their work. If you don't train your staff, and keep on doing so, then you can't expect that level of excellence from them that you need.

It works both ways; you get more effective, efficient staff and their job satisfaction increases as they are rewarded with a greater sense of contribution to your business.

It's also important to make it clear that training is a reward and not a punishment. Don't present it to your staff as something they have to do because they are not performing adequately; make it clear that training is for those who deserve the chance to earn more, and be more successful. It's not about correcting their mistakes or behaviour; it's about developing their abilities to the fullest.

Your Staff Will Thrive If You Give Them Autonomy And Authority

You are in business because you love having the freedom to make your own decisions – and so do your staff. No one likes being checked up on all the time but sadly many business owners and entrepreneurs believe only they know how to do a job so they end up doing the very thing to their staff that they dislike the most! We know this from personal experience, because it is just what we did. Trusting your staff to do their job is essential, and if you have given them the right training then they will do it. Monitoring what they do is one thing, and that is necessary, but constantly checking up on their work is not a productive use of your time and resources.

After you have trained your staff, you must give them the freedom to do what you have employed them to do. You must also give them autonomy and authority to carry out their job roles or you will risk losing them.

Why are you in business? To provide the highest level of service, benefit and result to the people who enquire, ask for advice and buy from you. How are you going to achieve that? By giving your staff the autonomy and authority that they need to do that without checking that they have done the right thing every five minutes. If you want to transform talented and extraordinary staff into superstars, then that's exactly the environment you must create for them.

Rewarding Performance

Business is based on results and, as we just mentioned, you need to monitor your staff's performance on a continuous basis. It's not about harassing them and chasing them for results; it's about having a relationship with them that makes it clear your objective is to get the best outcome for you, and for them. You need to be in constant contact in order to do this, and you must make it a priority to manage their results through encouragement, incentives, thanks and a very clear reward system.

Go into any infant school and you will see the perfect model for this. Children get awarded with gold stars for all aspects of their schoolwork and behaviour, and it's done publicly in front of the class or school so they get a real sense of pride at being recognised and rewarded for their achievements. They can get stars for academic success like being top in spelling, but they also get stars for being helpful, so they get a real sense that whatever they do – if they do it to the best of their ability – they can be rewarded. It works for them, and it will work for you and your staff because everyone likes to be appreciated and to see their efforts publicly rewarded. It is not about money as much as it is about pride in what they do, and you will see the results in increased effectiveness and performance across the board.

If the boss says you have done a good job, it means something, so never miss an opportunity to praise and reward someone's work, or their attitude. Make it clear to your staff what you expect from them and encourage them by the most effective means you have to consistently produce excellent work for you. Encourage them further to produce exceptional and outstanding work and to perform at their absolute best. When you have high expectations of them, they will have equally high expectations of themselves and everyone benefits.

CHAPTER 7

How To Prime Your Business For Top Flight Results

"If you do build a great experience, customers tell each other about that. Word of mouth is very powerful."
Jeff Bezos – Amazon.com Founder

The final chapter is about learning how to position your business so you are recognised as the expert and trusted advisor in your field. You are going to learn how to find more customers and turn them into brand evangelists.

Becoming an expert and trusted advisor is essential in today's competitive marketplace, because once you are positioned as such, you gain the trust and acceptance of your customers. From that position, you no longer sell to your customers but, instead, they come to you looking to buy.

Customers are skeptical about being sold to, but they are very open to being informed, advised and educated. Which approach do you think will make them trust you more – a hard sell, or outlining the benefits, and indeed any potential disadvantages, to them? It's all about that exceptional customer service, not selling them what you have, but letting them tell you what they need. Once you have their trust and confidence they are far more willing to buy from you, and to recommend you. This may seem like turning conventional sales wisdom on its head, and it is, but it works. The more information you give your customer then the more they will be drawn to ask you questions, and your advice. This gives you a huge advantage over your competitors and promotes a sense of integrity and trust in your business – and that's a big step towards being the market leader.

Isn't it crazy to tell your customers that your product isn't ideal for them and that your competitor has something more suited to their needs? No, because first of all if you sell them an unsuitable product you have set yourself up for after sales grief, and secondly they will appreciate your honesty and impartiality. That again positions you as the expert and trusted advisor in your marketplace, because you know your own and your competitors' products and are able to outline their respective advantages and disadvantages. Customers respond to, and respect, that approach and if you don't get that sale, they will come back to you in the future. They will also tell others about your honesty and good advice. That is good marketing, as opposed to ineffective selling, and will bring you to the attention of your target market as effectively as any other method.

What Do You Know?

It is surprising how many businesses are based on instinct, hunches and 'a feeling'. All of those are useful, but none of them can compete with doing research to see if you have a viable product or service in a profitable market. Just because you *think* you have a winning idea doesn't make it so; you must test both the product or service itself and the market niche you want to sell it in. If you don't, you may stand to lose time and financial resources. Go and ask people for their opinion but remember that friends and family will usually tell you what you want to hear simply because they are biased. Strangers have no reason to lie to you. If there is already an established market make sure you go and research it first. You may research in a number of ways but before you launch any business or a new product or service make sure you consider the following points:

- Can you make a sufficient margin on your product or service to make it profitable?

- How are your competitors marketing their own, similar, products or services to your target market?

- What is the 'unique selling point' that sets your product or service apart from anything else on the market?

- Can you see a niche within your target market that no one else is supplying?

- Is that niche likely to be able to provide a sufficient profit at present?

- Does that niche have potential for growth?

- What proportion of that niche will you need to capture to go past your break even point into profit?

- Is your market or niche crowded with too many competitors?

- What are your competitors doing to attract their customers?

- What is your cost to generate one customer?

- Do you know your customer lifetime value?

- Does your target market have the money to buy your product or service?

Research is essential to the success of your business. If you don't ask these basic questions you are setting yourself up for some expensive mistakes. Trying to sell a product that no one wants to buy in sufficient quantities to make it profitable is a recipe for disaster. As is trying to sell a high-ticket item to a market that has a low income; for instance, students do buy things but they are not in the market usually for fine vintage wines or antiquarian books. By clearly defining your market and its potential you are basing your future marketing plans on solid evidence, not gut feelings, you can then plan for a profitable future – not just hope for success.

Your Marketing Plan

Once you know who your customers are, and what they want, you have the bones of your marketing plan. It's an essential tool that will show you how and where to find your customers, and what strategy and techniques to use to sell to them. It's the most effective way to make sure you are driving the right customers to you or your sales team to maximise your chances of success.

Set clear goals, such as 10 sales a day, or a new product in 3 months, and make a timeline plan of how you are going to achieve that. For instance, if you want 10 sales a day from launch in a month's time then you start from the launch date and work backwards on the tasks that need to be done to get you there. It's no good starting the day before the launch to attract those customers, you need to have your adverts, your brochures, whatever techniques you are using already in place. Use your market research to help you formulate your goals and then keep using research to check whether your marketing is working or not. Do not take anything on trust. Check, check and check again. If you don't have this constant referral to the results you are getting, you are just wasting both time and money.

Focus On Your Customer

No product is universal, except perhaps a bottle of water and even there you have choice preferences for still, sparkling or flavoured. The moral? Don't try and sell to a very broad market. Go back to your market research and really focus in on who is your perfect customer. What do they most want and how does your product or service perfectly fit the bill? The result: you'll increase your sales and save money and time.

- Why do they need your product or service?
- What are their problems and how will your product solve them?
- What specific benefits are they looking for and how can you help them solve their problem with your product or service?
- What is it that will press the 'buying button' for them and has your research told you how to do that?

Customers buy for a whole variety of reasons and you must know what your target market is looking for. It could be prestige, price, effectiveness or something else but you won't get that sale unless you fulfil their own personal reasons - and you can't do that unless you know what they are.

Don't Get Complacent

It's easy to set up a marketing campaign and then forget about it as soon as it brings you in some results. It's working, so why bother with it? Because if you don't you are going to feel the effects once sales start slowing down. Pay attention on a daily basis and do something every day to promote your campaign, even if it's just 5 minutes thinking about what to do next it will contribute to your long term success.

If your campaign is so successful it brings in more sales than you can handle, you need to have a system in place to deal with it. Plan to be successful and visualise all possible outcomes of each campaign. Can you service that number of sales? If not, what are you going to do to make it happen? We are not saying take on extra staff in case you need them, but look at what other strategies you might need to employ. Could you outsource your packing for instance, or your accounts if needed? Are there areas you are not as effective in and that take up too much of your time? If so, look at getting someone else to do that, part time at first and see how the business develops.

You are in charge and it's your responsibility to make your business perform effectively, efficiently, and at its best so have a plan in place, don't just hope you can cope. If your marketing campaign brings in 100 enquiries you must know how you are going to handle them before your campaign launches. If you 'lose' customers because it takes you 3 days to answer an email then that is wasteful, in fact it's almost criminal, so streamline your process for dealing with it – and test it to make sure it works.

Also have a system for following up all enquiries; they may not buy from you now but they are your future market and you must stay in touch with them. Today's enquirer could be tomorrow's customer, so don't neglect them. And speaking of neglect, it's also all too easy to take your established customers for granted while you're actively seeking out new ones. Don't make that mistake, because the investment in a current customer will pay dividends – after all, they have already bought from you and therefore more likely to buy again. It's not cost effective to use your time and money to pursue new prospects at the expense of your old ones.

Do What Works, And Do It Again

Your market research, and sales, will tell you whether a specific marketing strategy is working and then what you need to do to keep repeating it. Don't be tempted to try something different just for the sake of it, you are far better to repeat a successful formula until you see it isn't working as well.

Consistency is the key, take your most successful webpage and add a few more testimonials. Test whether that makes a difference to sales, and if it does then try testing another element such as your bonus or special offer – make it bigger and see what result that brings in. We are talking about building on the success of your winning marketing idea by slowly increasing the elements, or the size, just one thing at a time and then monitoring the results. If it works, then keep it and try the next small change. If it doesn't, take that change out and test something else.

Remember those SMART goals we talked about earlier? Well it also applies to your marketing which has to fulfil those same criteria in order to get the same results. You want your campaign to be specific, measurable, achievable, realistic and time oriented – do this and you will soon see results.

Front End Versus Back End Marketing

We have already talked about how important it is that you don't offer your customer just one product. That initial sale and how you offer it is the front end of your marketing strategy, but the real profit in business is in back end marketing. That is the additional sales you will make after that initial one, and hopefully go on making to that customer.

We can't stress enough that you must have an effective back end strategy in place before you ever offer a product for sale.

Sell them one product and you have made a sale, continue to sell to them and you have made a customer for life. What you must do is offer excellent value to attract your prospects so that they make that first purchase with you, and then use your back end strategy to get them to spend more money with you in the future. For example, you may make little profit on the front end, but a lot from selling them a course on learning how to use that product, or offer a complementary product at a reduced price.

From all we have discussed so far, you have the knowledge of how to retain customers; with great service, reliable and consistent products. But you have to get those customers to you first by making a great initial offer, and then making sure they stay with you by having continuous, attractive offers to regularly sell to them. You will see how fast your business profits grow when you focus your attention on that back end.

Think of it from the point of view of you as a customer, as opposed to a business owner. Ever bought a piece of software that seems like a reasonable purchase? That company is probably losing money on it, but they now have you as a customer and other irresistible offers flow thick and fast and you probably take up at least one or two of them. If they really market to you, then they will be offering you products that will enhance the one you have, or are related in some way. They aren't bombarding you with irrelevant and useless products, but they have studied what you have purchased and targeted their back end offers to that. And it works doesn't it?

Marketing And Your Customers

The point of all this marketing is obviously to make sales and be in profit. We have discussed the various ways you can do that, and now we want to just really examine how your understanding of your primary purpose will dictate your ultimate success or failure.

All companies make great promises, but very few actually fulfil them. If you are one of the latter then your customers rely on you and will give you their future custom, often over many years. However, in order to stay in business you have to attract new customers. How do you do that and retain your loyal customer base? Simply by treating each group separately and using different marketing strategies for each. Your established customers already trust you, so you don't have to spend time trying to build that with them, whereas with your new customers that is the key priority. Don't think one marketing campaign will fit both groups, it won't and you are likely to miss the target in both areas.

Your new customers need to be enticed with great offers and benefits from buying from you. We have already outlined some of the ways for you to help them choose to buy from you. When they experience your great product, service and reliability then they are converted to become established customers. However, your current list of customers already knows, likes and trusts you. They want the same level of service, they know you deliver what you promise, so they don't need persuading how good you are in quite the same way.

New customers can be attracted with a great initial offer, maybe a reduced price or an extra product at a low or no cost to them. You may not make a large profit on that initial sale but what you have got is a well targeted customer who is going to be very profitable over the long-term. You won't make much money from just one sale, but, once that sale is done, they have become more ready to be offered other products at more profit because they are now established customers who trust you.

Now you can devote your time and effort to nurturing what is the most profitable part of your business – your established customers. They are the backbone of long-term business success so treat them well and they will amply reward you.

If you want more profitable ideas to lead your business to spectacular success, we have lots of powerful marketing and promotion strategies collated and explained in our business marketing book.
You can get a copy from: www.businessmarketingbook.com.

Conclusion

We believe – and we hope – you now understand how to make your business a roaring success. Embrace this knowledge with an open mind so that you can apply it to your own business.

If you do so, then your business will be in a great position to survive and thrive and become the leader in your field, a respected and trusted provider.

No matter what the state of the economy, or how many competitors you have, you are in a position to become successful and wealthy as a direct result of your relentless focus on the primary purpose for being in business.

Remember, you and your business exist to provide the highest level of service, benefit and result to the people who enquire, ask for advice and buy from you.

Seize your opportunity!

Tell Us About Your Success

We would love to hear of your successes using the strategies, philosophies and methods in this book.

Send your story to: success@howtogrowabusiness.co.uk

We may contact you to find out more and feature you and your story in future editions of this book and our business success newsletters.